Natural Habitat of Fahaka Pufferfish

Overview

The Fahaka Pufferfish (Tetraodon lineatus), also known as the Nile Pufferfish, is a freshwater species known for its distinctive appearance and aggressive nature. Understanding its natural habitat is crucial for those interested in keeping these fascinating fish in captivity.

Geographical Distribution

Africa

The Fahaka Pufferfish is native to the freshwater systems of Africa. They are commonly found in the Nile River and other major river basins such as the Chad, Niger, Volta, and Gambia rivers.

Habitat Characteristics

Water Conditions

Fahaka Pufferfish thrive in warm, slow-moving waters. They prefer temperatures ranging from 75 to 82°F (24 to 28°C) and a pH level between 7.0 and 8.0. These conditions are typically found in large rivers, lakes, and floodplains.

Environment

These fish are often found in areas with abundant vegetation and soft substrates. They enjoy hiding places created by submerged plants, roots, and fallen branches, which provide them with shelter and hunting grounds.

Behavior and Adaptations

Diet

In their natural habitat, Fahaka Pufferfish are carnivorous, feeding on a variety of prey including mollusks, crustaceans, and smaller fish. Their strong beaks are adapted for cracking open hard shells, making them effective hunters.

Territorial Nature

Fahaka Pufferfish are highly territorial and solitary creatures. They are known to defend their territory aggressively against intruders, which is an important consideration for those keeping them in home aquariums.

Conservation Status

Currently, the Fahaka Pufferfish is not listed as endangered. However, habitat destruction and pollution pose threats to their natural environments. Conservation efforts are necessary to ensure the sustainability of their populations in the wild.

Physical Characteristics of Fahaka Pufferfish

General Appearance

The Fahaka Pufferfish (Tetraodon lineatus) is notable for its unique and striking appearance, which sets it apart from many other freshwater fish species.

Size and Shape

Adult Size

Fahaka Pufferfish can grow quite large, reaching lengths of up to 18 inches (45 cm) in captivity. In the wild, they may grow even larger under optimal conditions.

Body Shape

These fish have a robust, elongated body that tapers towards the tail. Their bodies are somewhat cylindrical, giving them a strong, torpedo-like appearance.

Coloration and Patterns

Body Color

The Fahaka Pufferfish displays a variety of colors, primarily shades of brown, yellow, and grey. Their coloration helps them blend into their natural surroundings in the wild.

Stripes and Markings

One of the most distinctive features of the Fahaka Pufferfish is the series of dark vertical stripes running along their bodies. These stripes provide effective camouflage in their natural habitats, especially among vegetation and submerged debris.

Defensive Mechanisms

Inflation

Like other pufferfish, the Fahaka Pufferfish can inflate its body by ingesting water or air. This defense mechanism makes it appear larger and more intimidating to potential predators.

Spines

When inflated, small spines become visible on the surface of the Fahaka

Pufferfish's body. These spines add an additional layer of defense, making it difficult for predators to swallow them.

Teeth and Beak

Beak Structure

The Fahaka Pufferfish has a strong, beak-like structure formed by the fusion of its teeth. This beak is capable of crushing hard shells of mollusks and crustaceans, which make up a significant portion of its diet.

Continuous Growth

The teeth of the Fahaka Pufferfish grow continuously throughout its life. To prevent overgrowth, these fish need to gnaw on hard objects, which helps to wear down their teeth naturally.

Eyes and Vision

Eye Position

Fahaka Pufferfish have large, prominent eyes located on the sides of their heads. This positioning gives them a wide field of vision, which is beneficial for spotting both prey and predators.

Color Vision

Research suggests that pufferfish, including the Fahaka Pufferfish, have good color vision. This ability aids in identifying food sources and navigating their environment.

Ideal Water Conditions for Fahaka Pufferfish

Temperature

Maintaining the right temperature is crucial for the health and well-being of Fahaka Pufferfish.

Optimal Temperature Range

The ideal water temperature for Fahaka Pufferfish is between **75°F and 82°F (24°C and 28°C)**. Consistent temperatures within this range mimic their natural habitat and promote good health.

Temperature Stability

Fahaka Pufferfish are sensitive to sudden changes in temperature. It is important to ensure a stable temperature to avoid stress and potential health issues.

pH Levels

The pH level of the water affects the overall health of Fahaka Pufferfish.

Optimal pH Range

Fahaka Pufferfish thrive in water with a pH level between **7.0 and 8.0**. This range replicates the slightly alkaline conditions of their natural river habitats.

Monitoring and Adjusting pH

Regularly monitor the pH levels using a reliable test kit. If adjustments are needed, use appropriate aquarium products to maintain the desired pH range.

Water Hardness

Water hardness is another important factor to consider for the well-being of Fahaka Pufferfish.

General Hardness (GH)

The recommended general hardness for Fahaka Pufferfish is between **8 to 15 dGH**. This ensures the water contains the necessary minerals for their health.

Carbonate Hardness (KH)

The carbonate hardness should be maintained between **10 to 20 dKH**. Proper

KH levels help stabilize the pH and prevent sudden fluctuations.

Water Filtration and Quality

Maintaining high water quality is essential for the health of Fahaka Pufferfish.

Filtration System

Use a high-quality filtration system capable of handling the bioload of Fahaka Pufferfish. A combination of mechanical, chemical, and biological filtration is recommended.

Regular Water Changes

Perform regular water changes, replacing 25-50% of the tank water weekly. This helps to remove toxins and maintain optimal water conditions.

Additional Considerations

Oxygenation

Ensure adequate oxygenation of the water by using air stones or surface agitation devices. *Fahaka Pufferfish require well-oxygenated water to thrive.*

Substrate and Decor

Provide a soft, sandy substrate and plenty of hiding places using rocks, driftwood, and plants. This mimics their natural environment and reduces stress.

Diet and Feeding Habits of Fahaka Pufferfish

Natural Diet

In the wild, Fahaka Pufferfish have a varied diet that primarily consists of meaty foods.

Primary Food Sources

Their natural diet includes:

- **Mollusks:** Snails, clams, and other shelled creatures.
- **Crustaceans:** Crabs, shrimp, and similar species.
- **Fish:** Smaller fish that they can catch.

Hunting Behavior

Fahaka Pufferfish are active hunters, using their strong beaks to crush the shells of mollusks and crustaceans. They rely on their keen eyesight to spot and capture their prey.

Feeding in Captivity

To maintain the health of Fahaka Pufferfish in captivity, it is essential to replicate their natural diet as closely as possible.

Dietary Requirements

In captivity, their diet should include a variety of meaty foods to ensure they receive all necessary nutrients. Suitable food items include:

- **Live or Frozen Foods:** Snails, shrimp, crabs, and small fish.
- **Prepared Foods:** Commercially available frozen foods such as krill, mussels, and cockles.

Feeding Schedule

Fahaka Pufferfish should be fed 2-3 times a week. Overfeeding can lead to health issues, so it's important to monitor their intake and ensure they are not being overfed.

Special Considerations

Beak Maintenance

The continuous growth of their teeth (or beak) requires special attention. Providing hard-shelled foods like snails and clams helps to naturally wear down their teeth and prevent overgrowth.

Variety and Enrichment

Offering a variety of foods not only ensures balanced nutrition but also provides mental stimulation. Live foods, in particular, can encourage natural hunting behaviors, enriching their captive environment.

Feeding Tips

Food Preparation

Thoroughly rinse live and frozen foods before feeding to remove any potential contaminants. For frozen foods, thaw them properly to ensure they are at the appropriate temperature for consumption.

Observation

Regularly observe your Fahaka Pufferfish during feeding to ensure they are eating properly and not exhibiting signs of stress or illness. Adjust their diet as needed based on their health and behavior.

Breeding Behavior of Fahaka Pufferfish

Introduction

Breeding Fahaka Pufferfish (Tetraodon lineatus) in captivity is a challenging task that requires specific conditions and careful attention. Understanding their breeding behavior is essential for success.

Natural Breeding Environment

Spawning Season

In the wild, Fahaka Pufferfish typically breed during the rainy season when water levels rise, creating optimal conditions for spawning and raising fry.

Nesting Sites

Fahaka Pufferfish prefer to lay their eggs in sheltered areas with abundant vegetation or submerged structures. These sites provide protection for the eggs and newly hatched fry.

Breeding in Captivity

Tank Setup

To encourage breeding in captivity, it is important to replicate their natural environment as closely as possible.

- **Tank Size:** A large tank of at least 100 gallons is recommended to provide ample space for the pair and their offspring.
- **Substrate:** Use a soft, sandy substrate to mimic their natural habitat.
- **Vegetation:** Provide plenty of live plants, rocks, and hiding places to create a suitable breeding environment.

Water Conditions

Maintain optimal water conditions to promote breeding:

- **Temperature:** Keep the water temperature between 75°F and 82°F (24°C and 28°C).
- **pH Level:** Ensure the pH is between 7.0 and 8.0.
- **Water Quality:** Perform regular water changes to maintain high water quality.

Breeding Behavior

Courtship

During courtship, the male Fahaka Pufferfish displays vibrant colors and may engage in elaborate swimming patterns to attract the female. He may also create a nest by digging in the substrate and arranging vegetation.

Spawning

Once the female is ready to spawn, she will lay her eggs in the nest prepared by the male. The male then fertilizes the eggs. A single spawning can result in hundreds of eggs.

Egg Care

After fertilization, the male typically guards the eggs, protecting them from potential threats. The eggs usually hatch within a week, depending on water temperature and conditions.

Raising Fry

Initial Care

Newly hatched fry are very small and require special care:

- **Feeding:** Initially feed the fry infusoria or commercially available liquid fry food. As they grow, transition them to freshly hatched brine shrimp and finely crushed flakes.
- **Water Quality:** Maintain pristine water quality with regular, gentle water changes to ensure the fry's health and growth.

Growth and Development

The fry grow rapidly and will need progressively larger tanks as they develop. Monitor their growth and separate them if necessary to prevent aggression and cannibalism.

Challenges and Considerations

Aggression

Fahaka Pufferfish are known for their aggressive nature, even towards potential mates. Careful observation is needed to ensure the safety of both the male and female during the breeding process.

Success Rate

Breeding Fahaka Pufferfish in captivity has a relatively low success rate due to their specific requirements and aggressive behavior. Patience and dedication are essential for those attempting to breed these unique fish.

Lifespan of Fahaka Pufferfish in Captivity

General Lifespan

The Fahaka Pufferfish (Tetraodon lineatus) is known for its relatively long lifespan when properly cared for in captivity.

Average Lifespan

On average, Fahaka Pufferfish can live for **10 to 15 years** in captivity. With optimal care, some individuals may even live longer, reaching up to 20 years.

Factors Affecting Lifespan

Water Quality

Maintaining high water quality is crucial for the longevity of Fahaka Pufferfish. Regular water changes, proper filtration, and monitoring of water parameters such as pH, temperature, and hardness are essential.

Diet and Nutrition

A balanced and varied diet is key to ensuring the health and longevity of Fahaka Pufferfish. Providing a diet that includes live, frozen, and prepared foods helps meet their nutritional needs and prevent health issues related to poor diet.

Tank Size and Environment

Fahaka Pufferfish require ample space to thrive. A large tank of at least 100 gallons is recommended. Providing a stimulating environment with hiding places, vegetation, and appropriate tank mates (if any) also contributes to their well-being.

Health Care

Regular observation and prompt treatment of any health issues are vital. Fahaka Pufferfish can suffer from common fish diseases such as ich, bacterial infections, and parasitic infestations. Early detection and appropriate treatment are crucial for their long-term health.

Signs of Aging

Physical Changes

As Fahaka Pufferfish age, they may show signs such as a decrease in activity levels, changes in coloration, and a slower growth rate. Regular health checks can help monitor these changes and ensure they receive appropriate care.

Behavioral Changes

Aging Fahaka Pufferfish might become less aggressive and more reclusive. Providing a comfortable and stress-free environment can help mitigate the impact of aging on their behavior.

Maximizing Lifespan

Consistent Care

Consistent and attentive care is essential for maximizing the lifespan of Fahaka Pufferfish. This includes maintaining stable water conditions, providing a balanced diet, and ensuring a suitable tank environment.

Stress Reduction

Minimizing stress is crucial for the overall health of Fahaka Pufferfish. Avoid sudden changes in their environment, handle them gently during tank maintenance, and ensure they have plenty of hiding places to feel secure.

Conclusion

With proper care and attention, Fahaka Pufferfish can live long and healthy lives in captivity. Understanding their needs and providing a suitable environment are key factors in ensuring their longevity and well-being.

Social Behavior of Fahaka Pufferfish

General Overview

The Fahaka Pufferfish (Tetraodon lineatus) is known for its distinctive and often aggressive social behavior. Understanding their social interactions is crucial for anyone considering keeping them in a home aquarium.

Territorial Nature

Solitary Behavior

Fahaka Pufferfish are inherently solitary creatures. They prefer to live alone and can become highly territorial if housed with other fish, including other Fahaka Puffers.

Territorial Aggression

These fish are known for their aggressive defense of their territory. They will aggressively chase and attack intruders, which can lead to significant injuries or even death of tank mates.

Compatibility with Other Fish

Tank Mates

Due to their aggressive and territorial nature, finding suitable tank mates for Fahaka Pufferfish can be challenging.

- **Species-Only Tanks:** The safest option is to keep Fahaka Pufferfish in a species-only tank.
- **Large, Non-Aggressive Fish:** In some cases, very large and non-aggressive fish may coexist, but close monitoring is essential.

Risk of Aggression

Introducing any new fish to a Fahaka Pufferfish's tank carries a high risk of aggression. It's important to provide ample space, hiding places, and visual barriers to minimize territorial disputes.

Interaction with Humans

Intelligent and Observant

Fahaka Pufferfish are intelligent and observant fish. They often recognize their owners and can become interactive during feeding times, displaying curious behaviors.

Handling Precautions

While they may show interest in their owners, Fahaka Pufferfish should not be handled directly. Their strong beaks can cause serious injury, and handling can also stress the fish.

Feeding Behavior

Predatory Instincts

Their feeding behavior reflects their predatory nature. Fahaka Pufferfish are active hunters and enjoy chasing and catching live prey, which can also serve as enrichment in captivity.

Feeding Response

They have a strong feeding response and can become excited during feeding times. It's important to monitor feeding to ensure all food is consumed and to prevent overfeeding.

Breeding Behavior

Increased Aggression

During breeding, Fahaka Pufferfish can become even more aggressive. Males will defend their nesting sites vigorously, and careful observation is needed to ensure the safety of both fish during this period.

Parental Care

In some cases, male Fahaka Pufferfish exhibit parental care by guarding the eggs until they hatch. This behavior, however, can vary among individuals.

Conclusion

Understanding the social behavior of Fahaka Pufferfish is essential for their care. Their territorial and aggressive nature makes them best suited for solitary living or carefully monitored environments with appropriate tank mates. Providing an enriching environment and respecting their space can help maintain their health and well-being in captivity.

Size and Growth Rate of Fahaka Pufferfish

Adult Size

Fahaka Pufferfish (Tetraodon lineatus) are known for their impressive size, especially compared to other freshwater pufferfish species.

Maximum Length

In captivity, Fahaka Pufferfish can reach up to **18 inches (45 cm)** in length. In their natural habitat, they may grow even larger under optimal conditions.

Growth Rate

The growth rate of Fahaka Pufferfish can vary based on several factors, including diet, tank conditions, and overall care.

Juvenile Growth

Young Fahaka Pufferfish typically grow rapidly during their first year. With proper nutrition and care, they can reach **6 to 8**

*inches (15 to 20 cm) within the first 12
months.*

Continued Growth

*After the initial rapid growth phase, their
growth rate slows down but remains steady.
They can continue to grow slowly for several
more years until they reach their full adult
size.*

Factors Influencing Growth

Diet and Nutrition

*A varied and nutritious diet is crucial for
the healthy growth of Fahaka Pufferfish.
Providing a diet rich in protein, including live,
frozen, and prepared foods, supports their
growth and overall health.*

Tank Size and Environment

*Providing ample space is essential for
their growth. Fahaka Pufferfish require large
tanks, at least 100 gallons, to accommodate
their size and allow for proper swimming and
exploration.*

Water Quality

Maintaining optimal water conditions, including stable temperature, pH, and cleanliness, is vital for promoting healthy growth. Poor water quality can stifle growth and lead to health issues.

Monitoring Growth

Regular Measurements

Regularly measuring and recording the size of your Fahaka Pufferfish can help monitor their growth and ensure they are developing properly. This can also help identify any potential health issues early on.

Signs of Healthy Growth

Healthy Fahaka Pufferfish should exhibit consistent growth, vibrant coloration, and active behavior. A well-balanced diet and a clean, spacious tank contribute to these positive indicators.

Conclusion

Understanding the size and growth rate of Fahaka Pufferfish is essential for their care.

With proper nutrition, a suitable environment, and careful monitoring, these fascinating fish can reach their full potential and thrive in captivity.

Common Tank Mates for Fahaka Pufferfish

Introduction

Fahaka Pufferfish (Tetraodon lineatus) are known for their aggressive and territorial nature, making it challenging to find suitable tank mates. However, with careful selection and monitoring, it is possible to keep them with other fish under the right conditions.

Best Practices for Choosing Tank Mates

When selecting tank mates for Fahaka Pufferfish, consider the following factors:

- **Size:** Choose larger fish that are not easily perceived as prey.
- **Temperament:** Opt for non-aggressive species to avoid provoking the Fahaka Pufferfish.
- **Tank Size:** Ensure the tank is large enough (at least 100 gallons) to provide ample space and reduce territorial aggression.
- **Habitat:** Provide plenty of hiding spots and visual barriers using plants, rocks, and decorations to help reduce stress and territorial disputes.

Potential Tank Mates

Large, Peaceful Fish

While no tank mate is guaranteed to be safe with Fahaka Pufferfish, the following larger, peaceful fish are sometimes successfully kept together:

- **Large Cichlids:** Species such as Oscars and Severums may coexist due to their similar size and robustness.
- **Bichirs:** These bottom-dwelling fish are generally peaceful and can avoid confrontation.
- **Large Catfish:** Species like the Plecostomus or Synodontis catfish are often too large and armored to be seen as prey.

Invertebrates

Generally, invertebrates are not suitable tank mates for Fahaka Pufferfish, as they are likely to be viewed as food. However, in very large tanks with ample hiding spaces, some keepers have had success with:

- **Large Snails:** Only very large and tough species like the Giant Sulawesi Snail may survive.
- **Large Shrimp:** Species such as Amano Shrimp, though this is very risky.

Considerations and Cautions

Monitoring and Adjustment

Careful monitoring is essential when introducing any tank mates to a Fahaka Pufferfish. Be prepared to separate fish if aggression occurs. Have a backup plan, such as an additional tank, ready if needed.

Individual Differences

Fahaka Pufferfish have individual personalities, and what works for one may not work for another. Some Fahaka Pufferfish may never tolerate tank mates, while others might coexist peacefully with certain species.

Conclusion

Choosing tank mates for Fahaka Pufferfish requires careful consideration and a willingness to intervene if conflicts arise. While it is challenging to find suitable companions due to their aggressive nature, with the right approach and environment, it is possible to create a harmonious tank.

History of Fahaka Pufferfish in the Aquarium Hobby

Introduction

The Fahaka Pufferfish (Tetraodon lineatus), also known as the Nile Pufferfish, is a fascinating species that has gained popularity in the aquarium hobby over the years. Known for its distinctive appearance and intriguing behavior, this pufferfish has a unique place in the world of aquarists.

Early Introduction

Discovery and Initial Interest

The Fahaka Pufferfish was first described scientifically in the 19th century. Native to the freshwater systems of Africa, particularly the Nile River, its striking look and interesting behaviors quickly caught the attention of fish enthusiasts and researchers.

Early Challenges

Initially, keeping Fahaka Pufferfish in captivity posed significant challenges due to their specific needs and aggressive nature. Early aquarists struggled with providing adequate care, leading to mixed success in keeping these fish alive and healthy.

Growing Popularity

Improved Understanding

As knowledge about their natural habitat and requirements grew, so did the ability of hobbyists to successfully maintain Fahaka Pufferfish. Advances in aquarium technology and water management helped overcome many of the early challenges.

Unique Appeal

The unique appeal of Fahaka Pufferfish, including their intelligence, personality, and ability to recognize their owners, contributed to their growing popularity. Their distinct look and the challenge they present to experienced aquarists also made them a sought-after species.

Modern Keeping Practices

Specialized Care

Today, keeping Fahaka Pufferfish is more common among advanced aquarists who can meet their demanding care requirements. Understanding their need for large tanks, a varied diet, and careful management of tank mates has become standard practice.

Community Knowledge

The growth of online communities and resources has made information about Fahaka Pufferfish more accessible. Aquarists now share experiences, tips, and best practices, helping newcomers succeed in keeping these fish.

Impact on the Hobby

Influence on Tank Design

The need for spacious and well-decorated tanks to accommodate Fahaka Pufferfish has influenced tank design trends. Many aquarists now prioritize creating natural and enriching environments that mimic the fish's natural habitat.

Contribution to Fishkeeping Skills

Keeping Fahaka Pufferfish has contributed to the overall skill level of hobbyists. The complexity of their care demands a higher understanding of fish biology, water chemistry, and aquarium management, raising the bar for advanced aquarists.

Conclusion

The history of Fahaka Pufferfish in the aquarium hobby is a testament to the dedication and passion of fish enthusiasts. From early challenges to modern successes, these fascinating fish have carved out a unique niche, continuing to captivate and challenge aquarists around the world.

Setting Up a Tank for Fahaka Pufferfish

Introduction

Fahaka Pufferfish (Tetraodon lineatus) require specific tank conditions to thrive due to their size, dietary needs, and aggressive nature. Proper tank setup is crucial for their health and well-being.

Tank Size and Placement

Minimum Tank Size

A single Fahaka Pufferfish requires a tank of at least **100 gallons** to provide adequate space for swimming and territory. Larger tanks are recommended for optimal comfort and to accommodate their growth.

Tank Placement

Place the tank in a quiet area away from direct sunlight and heavy foot traffic. This helps reduce stress and maintain a stable environment.

Substrate and Decorations

Substrate

Use a soft, sandy substrate to mimic their natural habitat. Sand is gentle on their bodies and allows them to exhibit natural digging behavior.

Decorations

Include a variety of decorations such as rocks, driftwood, and plants to create hiding spots and visual barriers. This helps reduce stress and territorial aggression.

- **Rocks and Driftwood:** Provide caves and crevices for the fish to explore and hide.
- **Plants:** Use hardy, freshwater plants like Java Fern, Anubias, and Vallisneria. These plants can withstand the pufferfish's activity and add to the tank's natural look.

Water Parameters

Temperature

Maintain the water temperature between **75°F and 82°F (24°C and 28°C)**. Use a reliable heater and thermometer to ensure a stable temperature.

pH and Hardness

Fahaka Pufferfish prefer a pH range of **7.0 to 8.0** and moderate hardness. Regularly test the water and make adjustments as necessary.

Filtration and Aeration

Install a high-quality filtration system capable of handling the bioload of a large, messy eater. Ensure adequate water flow and oxygenation through proper aeration.

Lighting

Lighting Requirements

Provide moderate lighting to support plant growth and maintain a natural day-night cycle. Avoid overly bright lights, which can stress the fish.

Tank Cycling

Initial Cycling

Before introducing the Fahaka Pufferfish, cycle the tank to establish a healthy bacterial colony. This process can take 4-6 weeks. Monitor ammonia, nitrite, and nitrate levels to ensure the tank is fully cycled.

Ongoing Maintenance

Perform regular water changes (20-30% weekly) to maintain water quality. Clean the substrate and decorations as needed to prevent waste buildup.

Introduction of the Fahaka Pufferfish

Acclimation Process

Acclimate the Fahaka Pufferfish slowly to the new tank environment. Float the fish in its bag for 15-20 minutes to equalize temperatures, then gradually mix tank water into the bag over 30-45 minutes before release.

Monitoring

Closely monitor the fish during the first few weeks for signs of stress or illness. Ensure it is eating well and adjusting to its new environment.

Conclusion

Setting up a tank for Fahaka Pufferfish requires careful planning and attention to detail. By providing a spacious, well-decorated environment with stable water conditions, you can ensure the health and happiness of these fascinating fish.

2/2

Common Diseases of Fahaka Pufferfish

Introduction

Fahaka Pufferfish (Tetraodon lineatus) are susceptible to various diseases, particularly when kept in improper conditions or exposed to stress. Understanding common diseases and their symptoms is crucial for early detection and treatment.

Bacterial Infections

Symptoms

- **Fin Rot:** Degradation of fins, often with white or red edges.
- **Bacterial Ulcers:** Open sores on the body, sometimes with redness or inflammation.
- **Pop-eye:** Swelling and protrusion of one or both eyes.

Treatment

Administer antibiotics as prescribed by a veterinarian or fish health professional.

Improve water quality and ensure proper tank hygiene to prevent further infections.

Parasitic Infestations

Symptoms

- **Ich (White Spot Disease):** Small white spots on the skin and fins.
- **Flukes:** Excessive mucus production, scratching against objects.
- **Protozoan Infections:** Behavioral changes, loss of appetite, and visible parasites.

Treatment

Use appropriate anti-parasitic medications to target specific parasites. Quarantine affected fish to prevent spreading to other tank mates. Maintain good water quality and hygiene.

Fungal Infections

Symptoms

- **Cotton Wool Disease:** White, cotton-like growth on the skin or fins.
- **Mouth Fungus:** White patches or growths around the mouth.

Treatment

Treat with antifungal medications, ensuring they are safe for use with pufferfish. Improve water quality and hygiene to prevent fungal outbreaks.

Nutritional Deficiencies

Symptoms

- **Vitamin Deficiencies:** Lethargy, loss of color, poor growth.
- **Malnutrition:** Failure to thrive, skeletal deformities.

Treatment

Provide a varied diet rich in vitamins and minerals. Supplement with appropriate commercial foods to ensure balanced nutrition.

Preventive Measures

Quarantine New Fish

Always quarantine new fish before introducing them to the main tank to prevent the spread of diseases.

Maintain Water Quality

Regularly test and maintain optimal water parameters (temperature, pH, ammonia, nitrite, nitrate) to reduce stress and susceptibility to diseases.

Monitor Behavior

Observe fish daily for any changes in behavior, appetite, or physical appearance. Early detection can lead to timely treatment and better outcomes.

Conclusion

By understanding and addressing common diseases of Fahaka Pufferfish promptly, aquarists can help ensure the long-term health and well-being of these unique and captivating fish.

Signs of Stress in Fahaka Pufferfish

Introduction

Identifying signs of stress in Fahaka Pufferfish (Tetraodon lineatus) is crucial for maintaining their health and well-being in the aquarium environment. Stress can lead to various health problems if not addressed promptly.

Behavioral Signs

Increased Aggression

Fahaka Pufferfish may exhibit heightened aggression towards tank mates or even towards their own reflections in the glass. They may chase other fish or show territorial behavior.

Restlessness

Restlessness can manifest as excessive swimming, pacing, or erratic movements.

The fish may appear agitated and constantly on the move.

Hiding or Retreat

Stressed pufferfish may seek refuge in hiding spots, plants, or decorations more frequently than usual. They may become reclusive and avoid interaction.

Physical Signs

Loss of Appetite

Stress can lead to a decrease in appetite. If a Fahaka Pufferfish suddenly stops eating or shows disinterest in food, it may indicate underlying stress.

Color Changes

Coloration can become dull or pale due to stress. In some cases, stressed pufferfish may darken in color, showing heightened stress responses.

Erratic Swimming Patterns

Abnormal swimming patterns such as darting, spinning, or swimming near the water surface or bottom can indicate stress.

Environmental Causes

Water Quality Issues

High levels of ammonia, nitrite, or nitrate can stress Fahaka Pufferfish. Poor water conditions affect their health and should be monitored regularly.

Changes in Tank Environment

Introducing new tank mates, rearranging decorations, sudden changes in lighting, or loud noises can stress pufferfish. Gradual adjustments and minimizing disturbances help reduce stress.

Response and Treatment

Immediate Action

If signs of stress are observed, assess and address potential causes promptly. Test water parameters and make necessary adjustments. Ensure a stable environment and provide hiding spots.

Monitoring and Adjustment

Monitor the pufferfish closely for any improvement or worsening of symptoms. Adjust tank conditions and minimize stressors to promote recovery.

Conclusion

Recognizing signs of stress in Fahaka Pufferfish is essential for proactive care. By understanding their behaviors and responding to stress promptly, aquarists can help maintain a healthy and thriving environment for these unique fish.

Importance of Aquarium Plants for Fahaka Pufferfish

Introduction

Aquarium plants play a significant role in the well-being and environment of Fahaka Pufferfish (Tetraodon lineatus). Understanding their importance can help create a balanced and enriched habitat for these unique fish.

Natural Habitat Reflection

Visual and Behavioral Enrichment

For Fahaka Pufferfish, aquarium plants provide a sense of security and mimic their natural habitat. Plants offer hiding spots, shelter, and visual barriers that reduce stress and territorial aggression.

Water Quality and Stability

Biological Filtration

Live plants contribute to the biological filtration of the aquarium. They absorb nitrates, ammonia, and other waste products produced by the fish, helping to maintain water quality and reduce the frequency of water changes.

Oxygenation and Aeration

During photosynthesis, aquatic plants release oxygen into the water. This process enhances oxygen levels, crucial for the health and activity of Fahaka Pufferfish, especially in large tanks with potentially limited surface area for gas exchange.

Dietary and Behavioral Benefits

Natural Grazing and Exploration

Some Fahaka Pufferfish may nibble on soft-leaved plants as part of their natural behavior. Providing suitable plant species can fulfill their grazing instincts and provide mental stimulation.

Physical and Mental Health

Well-planted aquariums encourage natural behaviors, such as exploration and foraging, which contribute to the overall well-being and happiness of Fahaka Pufferfish.

Choosing Suitable Plants

Hardy and Compatible Species

Select robust freshwater plants that can tolerate pufferfish activity and water conditions. Examples include Anubias, Java Fern, Vallisneria, and Amazon Sword plants.

Planting Techniques

Secure plants properly in the substrate to prevent uprooting by the pufferfish. Use weights or anchors if necessary, especially in tanks with active fish.

Conclusion

Aquarium plants are not only decorative but also serve essential functions in the care of Fahaka Pufferfish. From enhancing water quality to providing behavioral enrichment, plants contribute significantly to creating a thriving and harmonious aquatic environment for these fascinating fish.

Compatibility of Fahaka Pufferfish with Other Fish Species

Introduction

Choosing suitable tank mates for Fahaka Pufferfish (Tetraodon lineatus) requires careful consideration due to their aggressive nature and specific requirements. While challenging, successful tank mates can be found with proper planning and management.

Factors to Consider

Size Compatibility

Select fish that are similar in size to Fahaka Pufferfish or larger. Larger fish are less likely to be seen as prey and can better withstand any aggressive behavior from the pufferfish.

Temperament

Opt for calm and non-aggressive species. Avoid fish that are known to be fin-nippers or territorial, as they may provoke the pufferfish.

Behavioral Considerations

Choose fish that are fast-swimming and can evade the pufferfish if necessary. Species that inhabit different water layers or have different activity times can also help reduce conflicts.

Suitable Tank Mates

Large Cichlids

Some large cichlids, such as Oscars (Astronotus ocellatus) and Severums (Heros severus), can coexist with Fahaka Pufferfish due to their robust size and temperament.

Other Large, Peaceful Fish

Species like Bichirs (Polypterus spp.) and certain large catfish (e.g., Plecostomus) are sometimes compatible with Fahaka Pufferfish in spacious tanks with plenty of hiding spots.

Species with Armor or Defensive Adaptations

Fish with protective armor, such as certain species of armored catfish (e.g., Corydoras), may be less vulnerable to aggression from Fahaka Pufferfish.

Avoidance of Certain Species

Small Fish and Invertebrates

Avoid small fish and delicate invertebrates as tank mates, as Fahaka Pufferfish may view them as food. Shrimp, snails, and small schooling fish are not suitable companions.

Aggressive or Territorial Fish

Species known for aggression, such as aggressive cichlids (e.g., Mbuna) or territorial fish like some types of freshwater eels, should not be kept with Fahaka Pufferfish.

Monitoring and Adjustment

Observation and Intervention

Monitor tank mates closely after introduction. Be prepared to separate fish if aggression or stress signs appear. Provide ample hiding places and visual barriers to reduce conflict.

Alternative Tank Arrangements

Consider keeping Fahaka Pufferfish alone or in a species-only tank to avoid compatibility issues altogether. This ensures their well-being without the risk of harming other tank inhabitants.

Conclusion

Finding compatible tank mates for Fahaka Pufferfish requires careful selection and monitoring. By choosing species that match their size, temperament, and behavior, aquarists can create a harmonious environment that promotes the health and happiness of all tank inhabitants.

Differences between Male and Female Fahaka Pufferfish

Introduction

Fahaka Pufferfish (Tetraodon lineatus) exhibit subtle differences between males and females, primarily related to their reproductive organs and sometimes behavior. These differences are not always visually apparent and require careful observation.

Reproductive Organs

Male

Male Fahaka Pufferfish typically have more prominent and elongated gonads during the breeding season. These gonads are located internally and are not externally visible under normal circumstances.

Female

Female Fahaka Pufferfish have shorter and rounder gonads compared to males. During breeding, female pufferfish may appear slightly plumper due to the presence of eggs in their ovaries.

Behavioral Differences

Courtship and Aggression

During courtship, male Fahaka Pufferfish may exhibit more active and aggressive behavior towards females or competing males. They may chase females and display courtship rituals.

Females, on the other hand, may show increased receptiveness or avoidance behaviors depending on their readiness to spawn.

Visual Differences (Coloration and Size)

Coloration

In some cases, male pufferfish may display slightly brighter or more vivid coloration, especially during courtship or aggressive displays. However, color differences between sexes can be subtle and vary among individuals.

Size

There are generally no significant size differences between male and female Fahaka Pufferfish, as sexual dimorphism in size is minimal or absent in this species.

Conclusion

While distinguishing between male and female Fahaka Pufferfish can be challenging without direct observation of their reproductive organs or behavior, understanding these differences can be useful for breeders and hobbyists interested in their natural behaviors and reproductive biology.

Recommended Tank Size for Fahaka Pufferfish

Introduction

The Fahaka Pufferfish (Tetraodon lineatus) is a large and active species that requires a spacious tank to thrive. Choosing the right tank size is crucial for their health, well-being, and long-term care.

Minimum Tank Size

General Recommendation

A single Fahaka Pufferfish should be housed in a tank with a minimum capacity of **100 gallons**. This size provides enough space for the pufferfish to swim freely, exhibit natural behaviors, and establish territories.

Considerations for Tank Size

Growth Potential

Since Fahaka Pufferfish can grow up to 18 inches (45 cm) in length, larger tanks are highly recommended to accommodate their potential size. More space also helps reduce aggression and territorial disputes.

Behavioral Needs

Fahaka Pufferfish are active swimmers and require ample space to explore their environment. Insufficient tank size can lead to stress, aggression, and health issues.

Additional Tips

Single Species Tank

Consider keeping Fahaka Pufferfish in a species-only tank to avoid compatibility issues with other fish species. This setup allows them to thrive without territorial disputes or competition for resources.

Tank Configuration

Provide plenty of hiding spots, caves, and plants to create a stimulating and secure environment. This helps reduce stress and encourages natural behaviors.

Conclusion

Choosing a suitable tank size is critical for the well-being of Fahaka Pufferfish. By providing a spacious and well-maintained environment, aquarists can ensure these fascinating fish thrive and display their full range of behaviors in captivity.

Importance of Water Filtration for Fahaka Pufferfish

Introduction

Effective water filtration is essential for maintaining optimal water quality and the health of Fahaka Pufferfish (Tetraodon lineatus). Understanding the importance of filtration helps create a suitable environment for these sensitive and sometimes aggressive fish.

Removal of Waste and Debris

Mechanical Filtration

Mechanical filtration systems, such as sponge filters, filter pads, or canister filters, remove physical debris and waste from the water column. This prevents particles from accumulating and polluting the aquarium, which can affect water quality and fish health.

Biological Filtration

Nitrification Process

Biological filtration is crucial for Fahaka Pufferfish as it breaks down harmful ammonia (produced from fish waste and decaying matter) into less toxic nitrites and finally into nitrates. Beneficial bacteria in the filter media and substrate perform this essential nitrification process.

Nitrate Removal

While nitrates are less harmful than ammonia and nitrites, high levels can still stress fish and compromise their health. Regular water changes and a well-maintained biological filter help keep nitrate levels in check.

Chemical Filtration

Adsorption of Impurities

Chemical filtration media, such as activated carbon or zeolite, adsorb dissolved organic compounds, medications, and other impurities from the water. This *improves water clarity and removes potential toxins that can harm Fahaka Pufferfish.*

Importance of Proper Filtration

Stable Water Parameters

Consistent and effective filtration maintains stable water parameters, including ammonia, nitrite, nitrate levels, pH, and oxygenation. This stability is crucial for minimizing stress and promoting the overall health of Fahaka Pufferfish.

Reduction of Disease Risks

Clean and well-filtered water reduces the likelihood of diseases caused by poor water quality, such as bacterial infections, parasites, and fungal outbreaks. Healthy fish are more resilient and less susceptible to stress-related illnesses.

Choosing the Right Filter

Capacity and Efficiency

Select a filtration system that matches the size of the tank and the bio-load of Fahaka Pufferfish. Consider factors such as flow rate, filter media compatibility, and ease of maintenance to ensure optimal performance.

Regular Maintenance

Perform routine maintenance, including cleaning filter media and replacing chemical filtration media as recommended by the manufacturer. Monitor filter performance and water quality to address any issues promptly.

Conclusion

Water filtration is not only essential for maintaining water clarity but also plays a critical role in the health and well-being of Fahaka Pufferfish. By investing in a reliable filtration system and maintaining proper maintenance practices, aquarists can create a thriving and sustainable environment for these fascinating fish.

Best Practices for Maintaining Water Quality for Fahaka Pufferfish

Introduction

Maintaining optimal water quality is crucial for the health and well-being of Fahaka Pufferfish (Tetraodon lineatus). Implementing best practices ensures a stable and healthy aquatic environment, reducing stress and susceptibility to diseases.

Regular Water Testing

Testing Parameters

Regularly test water parameters such as ammonia, nitrite, nitrate, pH, and temperature using reliable test kits. Monitoring these parameters allows you to detect and address fluctuations before they impact your pufferfish.

Frequency

Test water quality weekly, especially in newly established tanks or when making changes to the tank environment. More frequent testing may be necessary during cycling or when fish show signs of stress.

Water Changes

Schedule

Perform regular partial water changes of about 20-30% every 1-2 weeks, or as needed based on water test results. This helps remove accumulated toxins, replenishes essential minerals, and maintains stable water parameters.

Procedure

Use a siphon to vacuum debris from the substrate during water changes. Treat new water with a suitable conditioner to remove chlorine/chloramine and match temperature to the tank water before adding.

Proper Feeding Practices

Quality and Quantity

Feed Fahaka Pufferfish a balanced diet of high-quality foods to minimize waste and maintain water quality. Avoid overfeeding, which can lead to excess ammonia and nitrate production.

Feeding Schedule

Offer small, frequent meals throughout the day rather than large feedings. Monitor feeding behavior and adjust portions accordingly to prevent uneaten food from fouling the water.

Avoid Overcrowding

Stocking Density

Avoid overcrowding the tank to prevent excessive waste production and competition for resources. Fahaka Pufferfish are territorial and require ample space to reduce stress and aggression.

Compatibility

Choose tank mates carefully to minimize bio-load and maintain water quality. Avoid mixing species that produce a high amount of waste or have conflicting environmental requirements.

Monitor and Respond to Changes

Behavioral Observations

Observe Fahaka Pufferfish daily for changes in behavior, appetite, or appearance, which can indicate stress or health issues. Prompt action can prevent water quality problems from escalating.

Emergency Preparedness

Have necessary equipment and medications on hand for treating common fish ailments. Quarantine fish promptly if necessary to prevent spreading diseases and maintain overall tank health.

Conclusion

By implementing these best practices for maintaining water quality, aquarists can create a stable and healthy environment for Fahaka Pufferfish. Consistent monitoring, proper feeding, regular maintenance, and *thoughtful stocking contribute to the long-term well-being of these fascinating fish.*

Role of Lighting in a Fahaka Pufferfish Tank

Introduction

Lighting plays a crucial role in the overall well-being and behavior of Fahaka Pufferfish (Tetraodon lineatus) in an aquarium environment. Understanding how to manage lighting effectively helps create a suitable habitat for these fish.

Natural Simulation

Day-Night Cycle

Provide a consistent day-night cycle with 10-12 hours of light followed by 10-12 hours of darkness. This mimics the natural environment and helps regulate the biological rhythms of Fahaka Pufferfish.

Dim Lighting

Fahaka Pufferfish prefer subdued or dim lighting conditions. Bright lighting can cause *stress and discomfort, leading to increased hiding and reduced activity.*

Aquatic Plant Considerations

Plant Growth

If your tank includes live plants, choose low to moderate lighting levels that promote healthy plant growth without causing excessive algae blooms. Some aquatic plants, like Anubias and Java Fern, thrive in shaded areas.

Lighting Duration

Adjust lighting duration based on the needs of your plants. Consider using timers to maintain a consistent lighting schedule, ensuring plants receive adequate light for photosynthesis.

Behavioral Impact

Activity Patterns

Proper lighting helps regulate Fahaka Pufferfish activity patterns. Dim lighting encourages natural behaviors such as foraging, exploring, and interacting with tank mates.

Stress Reduction

Avoid sudden changes in lighting intensity or duration, as this can stress Fahaka Pufferfish. Gradual adjustments and maintaining a stable lighting schedule promote a stress-free environment.

Conclusion

Lighting in a Fahaka Pufferfish tank should be carefully managed to replicate natural conditions, support plant growth (if applicable), and promote fish health and natural behaviors. By providing suitable lighting conditions, aquarists can create a balanced and comfortable environment for these unique and active fish.

Best Substrates for a Fahaka Pufferfish Aquarium

Introduction

The choice of substrate in a Fahaka Pufferfish (Tetraodon lineatus) aquarium is important for both aesthetic appeal and practicality. The substrate should support plant growth (if applicable), maintain water quality, and accommodate the natural behaviors of these fish.

Suitable Substrate Types

Sand

Sand is one of the most recommended substrates for Fahaka Pufferfish. It is gentle on their delicate undersides and allows them to sift through it naturally, mimicking their behavior in the wild. Choose fine to medium-grain sand that is easy to clean and does not trap debris.

Smooth Gravel

Smooth gravel with rounded edges can also be suitable for Fahaka Pufferfish. It provides a natural look and allows for easy cleaning. Ensure the gravel is not too coarse to avoid injuring the pufferfish or damaging their delicate skin.

Bare Bottom

In some setups, aquarists opt for a bare bottom tank for easier maintenance and to prevent accumulation of debris. This setup is less common but can work well for Fahaka Pufferfish, especially in species-only tanks where aesthetics are less of a concern.

Considerations for Plant Growth

Substrate Fertility

If you plan to keep live plants in the tank, choose a substrate that supports plant growth. Consider adding root tabs or liquid fertilizers to enrich the substrate with essential nutrients, as Fahaka Pufferfish can uproot plants if not anchored securely.

Plant Compatibility

Ensure the substrate is compatible with the types of plants you intend to grow. Some plants, like Anubias and Java Fern, can thrive when attached to driftwood or rocks instead of being planted directly in the substrate.

Maintenance Tips

Regular Cleaning

Regardless of the substrate type, perform regular maintenance to remove debris and waste buildup. Use a gravel vacuum or siphon to clean the substrate during water changes, focusing on areas where food and waste tend to accumulate.

Monitoring Water Quality

Monitor water parameters closely to ensure the substrate does not contribute to ammonia or nitrate spikes. Adequate filtration and regular water changes help maintain water quality and support the health of Fahaka Pufferfish.

Conclusion

Choosing the right substrate for a Fahaka Pufferfish aquarium involves balancing aesthetic preferences with practical considerations for fish health and maintenance. By selecting a suitable substrate type and maintaining it properly, aquarists can create a comfortable and functional environment for these active and unique fish.

Signs of a Healthy Fahaka Pufferfish

Introduction

Recognizing signs of health in Fahaka Pufferfish (Tetraodon lineatus) is essential for monitoring their well-being and ensuring optimal care in the aquarium environment. Healthy pufferfish exhibit specific behaviors and physical characteristics indicative of their overall health.

Physical Signs

Smooth Skin

Healthy Fahaka Pufferfish have smooth, unblemished skin without lesions, sores, or signs of injury. Their skin should appear firm and free from any abnormal growths.

Clear Eyes

The eyes of a healthy pufferfish are clear and free from cloudiness or swelling. They should be bright and responsive to their surroundings.

Full and Rounded Body

A healthy Fahaka Pufferfish has a full and rounded body shape. They should not appear overly thin or emaciated, which can indicate malnutrition or health issues.

Vibrant Coloration

While individual coloration may vary, healthy pufferfish typically exhibit vibrant and consistent coloring. Dull or faded colors can be a sign of stress or poor health.

Behavioral Signs

Active Swimming

Healthy Fahaka Pufferfish are active swimmers, exploring their environment and interacting with tank mates (if compatible). They should exhibit normal swimming patterns without excessive hiding or lethargy.

Appetite and Feeding

A healthy pufferfish has a robust appetite and eagerly consumes food during feeding times. They should show interest in food offerings and actively hunt or forage for food items.

Interaction with Environment

Observing natural behaviors such as investigating tank decor, interacting with plants, and exploring hiding spots indicates a healthy Fahaka Pufferfish.

Maintenance and Care

Water Quality

Maintaining stable water parameters and performing regular water changes ensures a healthy environment for Fahaka Pufferfish. Clean, well-oxygenated water supports their overall health and reduces stress.

Observation and Monitoring

Regularly monitor the behavior, appearance, and appetite of Fahaka Pufferfish. Promptly address any changes or abnormalities to prevent potential health issues.

Conclusion

Recognizing the signs of a healthy Fahaka Pufferfish involves assessing both physical appearance and behavioral cues. By providing proper care, a suitable environment, and monitoring their well-being, aquarists can help ensure these fascinating fish thrive in captivity.

Methods to Enhance the Color of Fahaka Pufferfish

Introduction

Enhancing the color of Fahaka Pufferfish (Tetraodon lineatus) can be achieved through various methods that promote overall health, provide appropriate nutrition, and optimize environmental conditions. Vibrant coloration is often a sign of good health and vitality in these fish.

Optimal Water Quality

Water Parameters

Maintain stable water parameters within recommended ranges for Fahaka Pufferfish. This includes appropriate temperature, pH levels, and water hardness. Consistent water quality supports healthy skin pigmentation and overall color intensity.

Water Filtration

Effective filtration helps maintain water clarity and purity, reducing stress and allowing natural colors to show prominently. Clean, well-oxygenated water is essential for enhancing the coloration of Fahaka Pufferfish.

High-Quality Diet

Variety of Foods

Offer a diverse diet that includes high-quality protein sources such as live or frozen foods (e.g., bloodworms, brine shrimp), as well as commercial pufferfish pellets or flakes enriched with vitamins and minerals.

Supplements and Color Enhancers

Consider supplements or foods formulated specifically to enhance coloration in aquarium fish. Some products contain natural color enhancers like astaxanthin and beta-carotene, which can intensify reds, oranges, and yellows in pufferfish.

Lighting Considerations

Proper Spectrum

Provide appropriate lighting with a spectrum that enhances the natural colors of Fahaka Pufferfish. LED lighting systems often offer customizable settings to mimic natural sunlight, which can bring out the best colors in your fish.

Photoperiod

Maintain a consistent day-night cycle with appropriate lighting duration. This helps regulate biological rhythms and supports normal coloration in Fahaka Pufferfish.

Environmental Enrichment

Aquatic Plants and Decor

Include live plants and decorative elements in the aquarium to provide hiding spots and stimulation for Fahaka Pufferfish. Natural environments with plants can reduce stress and encourage natural behaviors, which can enhance color vibrancy.

Minimal Stress

Minimize stress factors such as sudden changes in water parameters, aggressive tank mates, or overcrowding. Stress can dull the colors of pufferfish, so creating a peaceful and suitable habitat is crucial for maintaining vibrant coloration.

Conclusion

Enhancing the color of Fahaka Pufferfish involves a combination of optimal care practices, high-quality nutrition, appropriate lighting, and environmental enrichment. By providing a healthy and stimulating environment, aquarists can help Fahaka Pufferfish display their full range of vibrant colors and thrive in captivity.

Challenges of Keeping Fahaka Pufferfish in a Community Tank

Introduction

Fahaka Pufferfish (Tetraodon lineatus) are known for their unique behaviors and specific care requirements, which can pose challenges when kept in a community tank with other fish species. Understanding these challenges is crucial for successful tank management and the well-being of all inhabitants.

Aggressive Behavior

Territorial Nature

Fahaka Pufferfish are highly territorial and can be aggressive towards tank mates, especially during feeding or when establishing their territory. They may chase or nip at other fish, leading to stress and potential injuries.

Bullying and Predation

Pufferfish have a strong predatory instinct and may view smaller tank mates as potential prey, particularly if they resemble invertebrates or smaller fish. This predatory behavior can result in injury or even death for more vulnerable species.

Dietary Requirements

Specialized Diet

Fahaka Pufferfish require a diet high in protein, including crustaceans, mollusks, and occasionally small fish. Their dietary needs may conflict with those of other fish in the community tank that require herbivorous or omnivorous diets.

Competitive Feeding

Pufferfish are competitive feeders and may outcompete slower or more timid tank mates for food. This can lead to malnutrition or stress in other fish that are unable to access sufficient food.

Space and Tank Size

Large Territory Requirements

Due to their territorial nature, Fahaka Pufferfish require ample space to establish territories and reduce aggression towards tank mates. Inadequate tank size can exacerbate aggression and stress among fish in a community setup.

Compatibility Issues

Choosing suitable tank mates that can tolerate the aggressive and territorial behaviors of Fahaka Pufferfish can be challenging. Many peaceful or small fish species are not compatible and may become targets of aggression.

Environmental Considerations

Water Quality

Managing water quality is more challenging in a community tank with Fahaka Pufferfish due to their higher waste production and specific dietary needs. Maintaining stable water parameters is crucial to prevent stress-related illnesses and maintain overall fish health.

Behavioral Management

Monitoring and managing aggressive behaviors and interactions among tank mates requires careful observation and intervention. Providing ample hiding spots and visual barriers can help mitigate aggression and reduce stress in the tank.

Conclusion

Keeping Fahaka Pufferfish in a community tank presents several challenges related to their aggressive behavior, dietary requirements, space needs, and compatibility issues with other fish species. Successful management involves careful planning, monitoring, and providing an environment that meets the specific needs of these unique fish.

Recommended Water Temperature Range for Fahaka Pufferfish

Introduction

Maintaining appropriate water temperature is crucial for the health and well-being of Fahaka Pufferfish (Tetraodon lineatus) in an aquarium environment. Understanding their temperature preferences helps create a stable and comfortable habitat.

Ideal Temperature Range

Temperature Range

The recommended water temperature range for Fahaka Pufferfish is typically between **24°C to 28°C (75°F to 82°F)**. This range closely mimics their natural habitat conditions and supports their metabolic processes and overall health.

Stable Temperature

It's important to maintain a stable water temperature within this range to prevent stress and fluctuations that can impact the immune system and behavior of Fahaka Pufferfish.

Temperature Considerations

Heating and Cooling

Use a reliable aquarium heater to maintain consistent water temperature, especially in regions with fluctuating room temperatures or during seasonal changes. Monitor temperature regularly to ensure it remains within the recommended range.

Avoid Extremes

Avoid sudden temperature fluctuations or extremes, as these can stress Fahaka Pufferfish and compromise their health. Gradual changes in temperature are preferable if adjustments are necessary.

Conclusion

By maintaining the recommended water temperature range and ensuring stability, aquarists can create a suitable environment for Fahaka Pufferfish to thrive. Monitoring temperature and responding to any deviations promptly contribute to the overall well-being of these unique and fascinating fish.

Behavior of Fahaka Pufferfish During Spawning

Introduction

Fahaka Pufferfish (Tetraodon lineatus) exhibit interesting behaviors during the spawning process, which involves courtship rituals, nest preparation, and parental care. Understanding their spawning behavior is essential for aquarists interested in breeding these fish.

Courtship and Pairing

Male Displays

During courtship, male Fahaka Pufferfish may display heightened activity and aggression towards potential mates. They may chase females and perform elaborate displays, including fin flaring and circling movements.

Female Response

Females may show initial resistance but eventually become receptive to the male's advances. They may respond by showing submissive behaviors or joining the male in ritualistic movements.

Nest Preparation

Mating Site Selection

Once paired, Fahaka Pufferfish select a suitable spawning site. They may clear an area or create a depression in the substrate where eggs will be deposited and guarded.

Egg Laying

Female pufferfish lay eggs in batches, which adhere to surfaces within the chosen spawning site. Eggs are typically transparent and adhesive, attaching to plants, substrate, or tank surfaces.

Parental Care

Male Guarding

After fertilization, the male Fahaka Pufferfish assumes the role of guarding the nest and eggs. He aggressively defends the territory against intruders and monitors the developing eggs.

Female Role

The female may assist in guarding the nest initially but tends to take a less active role compared to the male. Her involvement may vary depending on the individual pair dynamics.

Post-Spawning Behavior

Egg Development

Both parents continue to guard the eggs until they hatch, which typically occurs within several days depending on water temperature and conditions.

Rearing Fry

After hatching, Fahaka Pufferfish fry are initially transparent and require microscopic food such as infusoria or finely powdered commercial fry food. Parental care may continue during the early stages of fry development.

Conclusion

The spawning behavior of Fahaka Pufferfish involves intricate courtship rituals, nest preparation, and parental care by both male and female. Providing a suitable environment and monitoring their behavior during spawning can increase the likelihood of successful breeding in captivity.

Ways to Prevent Fahaka Pufferfish from Jumping Out of the Tank

Introduction

Fahaka Pufferfish (Tetraodon lineatus) are known to be skilled jumpers, which can pose a risk if they leap out of the aquarium. Implementing preventive measures is crucial to ensure their safety and well-being in captivity.

Covering the Tank

Secure Lid or Cover

Use a secure aquarium lid or cover that fits tightly on top of the tank. Ensure there are no gaps or openings through which the pufferfish can escape. Acrylic or glass lids are effective choices.

Customized Cover

If your tank has equipment or fixtures that require openings (e.g., filters, heaters), consider using a customized cover with openings for these elements while still preventing fish from jumping out.

Managing Water Level

Leave Adequate Space

Maintain the water level in the tank slightly below the top rim to discourage jumping behavior. Fahaka Pufferfish are less likely to attempt jumping if they cannot easily reach the top of the tank.

Adjust Tank Design

If possible, choose a tank design that has a lower profile or rimless style, which reduces the distance from the water surface to the top of the tank. This can discourage jumping behavior.

Behavioral Considerations

Minimize Stress

Avoid stressful conditions in the tank that may prompt Fahaka Pufferfish to jump, such as sudden changes in water parameters, aggressive tank mates, or loud noises near the aquarium.

Provide Hiding Spots

Include ample hiding spots and shelter within the tank. This allows the pufferfish to feel secure and reduces the likelihood of them attempting to escape due to perceived threats or stress.

Regular Monitoring

Inspect Tank Equipment

Regularly check the aquarium lid or cover for any signs of wear, damage, or gaps that may develop over time. Replace or repair as needed to maintain a secure barrier.

Observe Pufferfish Behavior

Monitor the behavior of Fahaka Pufferfish regularly. Look for signs of restlessness, pacing near the water surface, or repeated attempts to jump. Adjust tank conditions or cover accordingly to minimize escape risks.

Conclusion

Preventing Fahaka Pufferfish from jumping out of the tank involves proactive measures such as using a secure lid or cover, managing water levels, reducing stress factors, and providing appropriate tank design and hiding spots. By creating a safe and secure environment, aquarists can minimize the risk of escape and ensure the well-being of these active and curious fish.

Use of Live Food for Fahaka Pufferfish

Introduction

Live food plays a crucial role in the diet of Fahaka Pufferfish (Tetraodon lineatus), providing essential nutrients and stimulating their natural predatory behaviors. Understanding the benefits and considerations of feeding live food helps maintain the health and vitality of these unique fish.

Benefits of Live Food

Nutritional Value

Live foods such as live insects, crustaceans, and small fish are rich in proteins, vitamins, and minerals that are beneficial for Fahaka Pufferfish. They provide a varied diet that supports growth and overall health.

Natural Hunting Behavior

Feeding live food encourages natural hunting behaviors in Fahaka Pufferfish, which helps maintain their mental and physical stimulation. This activity mimics their natural feeding habits in the wild, promoting a more active lifestyle.

Types of Live Food

Insects and Worms

Common live foods for Fahaka Pufferfish include mealworms, crickets, earthworms, and other small insects. These can be gut-loaded with nutritious foods before feeding to enhance their nutritional value.

Crustaceans

Small crustaceans such as shrimp, krill, and crayfish are excellent sources of protein for Fahaka Pufferfish. They provide a natural prey option that stimulates hunting instincts.

Small Fish

Occasionally, Fahaka Pufferfish can be fed small live fish such as guppies, minnows, or feeder fish. Ensure these fish are of appropriate size and sourced from reputable suppliers to avoid introducing diseases.

Considerations for Feeding

Quality and Source

Ensure live foods are of high quality and free from parasites or contaminants. Avoid collecting live foods from potentially polluted environments to prevent health risks to the pufferfish.

Feeding Frequency

Offer live food as part of a varied diet for Fahaka Pufferfish. Balance live food with other nutritious options such as frozen foods, pellets, or vegetables to ensure a complete diet.

Feeding Techniques

Live Feeding Schedule

Plan a feeding schedule that includes live food sessions periodically to stimulate natural behaviors and provide enrichment for Fahaka Pufferfish. Monitor feeding behaviors and adjust quantities as needed.

Observation and Interaction

Observe pufferfish during feeding to ensure they consume live food without issues. Remove any uneaten live food promptly to maintain water quality and prevent potential health problems.

Conclusion

Live food enhances the diet of Fahaka Pufferfish by providing essential nutrients and promoting natural hunting behaviors. By incorporating a variety of live foods and observing feeding practices, aquarists can support the health and well-being of these fascinating fish in captivity.

History and Origin of the Fahaka Pufferfish Species

Introduction

The Fahaka Pufferfish (Tetraodon lineatus) is a species with an intriguing history and natural habitat that has captivated aquarists worldwide. Understanding its origins sheds light on its evolution and adaptation to various environments.

Natural Habitat

Geographical Distribution

Fahaka Pufferfish are native to freshwater habitats across Africa, primarily found in rivers and lakes spanning regions such as the Nile River basin, Lake Tanganyika, and Lake Victoria. They inhabit areas with slow-moving or stagnant water and dense vegetation.

Adaptation to Environment

Evolutionarily adapted to their environment, Fahaka Pufferfish have developed unique physiological features and behaviors to survive in diverse African ecosystems. Their ability to inflate their bodies as a defense mechanism against predators is a notable adaptation.

Discovery and Taxonomy

Scientific Classification

Tetraodon lineatus was formally described by the French naturalist Georges Cuvier in the early 19th century. The species belongs to the family Tetraodontidae, which includes various pufferfish species known for their ability to inflate their bodies.

Aquarium Introduction

Due to their distinctive appearance and interesting behaviors, Fahaka Pufferfish gained popularity in the aquarium trade. They were introduced to the hobbyists' market as enthusiasts sought to observe and care for these unique freshwater fish.

Conservation Status

Wild Population Challenges

While not currently classified under major conservation concern, wild populations of Fahaka Pufferfish face threats from habitat degradation, pollution, and overfishing in some regions of Africa. Conservation efforts aim to preserve their natural habitats and maintain biodiversity.

Captive Breeding

In captivity, Fahaka Pufferfish are bred for the aquarium trade under controlled conditions. Responsible breeding programs help reduce pressure on wild populations and promote sustainable practices within the aquaculture industry.

Conclusion

The Fahaka Pufferfish species has a rich history rooted in African freshwater ecosystems, where it has evolved unique adaptations for survival. Its journey from natural habitats to aquariums worldwide highlights its cultural and ecological significance, inspiring efforts to conserve and understand these remarkable fish.

Importance of Regular Tank Maintenance for Fahaka Pufferfish

Introduction

Regular tank maintenance is crucial for maintaining a healthy environment for Fahaka Pufferfish (Tetraodon lineatus) in captivity. Proper maintenance routines help prevent water quality issues, reduce stress, and promote overall well-being.

Water Quality Management

Monitoring Parameters

Regular water testing for pH levels, ammonia, nitrite, and nitrate concentrations is essential. Fahaka Pufferfish are sensitive to fluctuations in water quality, and maintaining stable parameters mimics their natural habitat conditions.

Water Changes

Schedule routine water changes to remove accumulated waste, toxins, and excess nutrients. Freshwater changes help dilute pollutants and maintain optimal water chemistry, reducing the risk of stress-related illnesses.

Tank Cleaning and Hygiene

Substrate Maintenance

Vacuum the substrate regularly to remove uneaten food, fish waste, and debris. This prevents the buildup of organic matter that can degrade water quality and create breeding grounds for harmful bacteria.

Filter Maintenance

Clean and maintain the aquarium filter according to manufacturer guidelines. A clean filter ensures efficient mechanical and biological filtration, essential for removing particulates and maintaining a healthy nitrogen cycle.

Health and Disease Prevention

Observation and Quarantine

Regularly observe Fahaka Pufferfish for signs of stress, illness, or abnormal behavior. Quarantine new fish before introducing them to the main tank to prevent the spread of diseases that can impact the entire aquarium population.

Hygiene Practices

Practice good hygiene when handling aquarium equipment, decor, and water. Avoid cross-contamination between tanks and ensure equipment is cleaned with aquarium-safe products to maintain a healthy environment.

Behavioral Enrichment

Environmental Stimuli

Rotate and enrich the tank environment with new plants, decor, or rearrangements. Provide hiding spots, caves, and natural structures to stimulate natural behaviors and reduce stress in Fahaka Pufferfish.

Feeding and Routine

Establish a consistent feeding schedule that meets the nutritional needs of Fahaka Pufferfish. Avoid overfeeding to prevent water pollution and maintain water quality.

Conclusion

Regular tank maintenance is essential for the health and well-being of Fahaka Pufferfish in captivity. By monitoring water quality, cleaning the tank and equipment, preventing diseases, and providing enrichment, aquarists can create a stable and thriving environment for these fascinating fish.

Made in United States
Troutdale, OR
07/22/2024

21469277R00066